BELIEVERS
TALKING THE TALK

Beverly O'Rourke

ISBN: 9798491259304

Printed in the United States of America

Published by Book Marketeers.com

"I am the light of the world; he that follow me shall not walk in darkness, but Shall have the light of life"

John 8:12

FOREWORD

I am not a minister, preacher, student of theology, or "Bible thumper". I don't pretend to be a good student of the Bible, nor do I pretend to understand the meaning of all the Scriptures. I don't pretend to be a good church person because for the last few years I visit the church when I feel like it. The coronavirus has kept me away some, while others manage to stay close to the church. At the same time, I do believe in God, and I do believe in love, faith, patience, and the covenant that God made to us. I believe that there is just too much talking the talk and too little walking the walk in the world today.

I wrote this book because I am tired of watching TV evangelists milking their audiences with prayer cloths, holy water, and dreams of obtaining wealth and prosperity if they only send money. I am tired of listening to people who like to preach and proclaim their love for God while they live a life full of hatred, bitterness, and violence. I write this book because people are spending more time praising the Lord in church then they spend playing ball with their children. They spend more time talking the talk than they do helping their elderly parents survive a few more years. They spend more time singing praises to the Lord than they do volunteering to help someone or some program, help others. Yes, they spend more time pretending to be good Christians than they do just trying to be good, decent, and moral people. Jesus was clear when he said in (Luke 6:49) "but he that heareth and doeth not, is like a man that without a foundation built a house upon the earth against which the stream did beat vehemently, and immediately it fails and the ruin of that house was great".

Did Jesus mean for us to spend our lives with our heads bowed in prayer? Did Jesus mean for us to spend our lives just reading and learning? Isn’t the point of it all, to do his will? Isn't the point of it all to go out and do what he commanded of us? Didn’t Jesus speak of marriage, family, children, and community? Should they take second in our time and efforts? What benefit to the world is derived from a person spending four to five hours sitting in church? Isn’t the benefit of sitting in church all day personal and for self?

I am just a human being who has a philosophy about life that I want to share. I believe that my philosophy can help answer many questions for those who have been lost and need to find a better way to live. But like sex and politics, religion is a “sacred cow”. We learn from an early age that we should never talk about sex, politics, and religion in public if we want to be liked in this world. People who step beyond those barriers are often branded stupid, heretical, or blasphemous, or worse, arrogant, presumptuous, and angry.

Many people might believe that without the white-collar around your neck, you have no right to voice your beliefs. That somehow the lack of a white-collar or title of minister, preacher, or religious teacher behind your name, makes you ineligible to speak. But my friend, religion is the very root of our existence as humans. Without it, we have no direction, no history, no sense of life goals, and an understanding of what and who we are. Religion is the very foundation of human being’s ability to live with each other. Even persons who oppose religion, have taken the time to find the reason for opposition to it. This in my mind simply connects them to it just as tightly as those who believe in it. Morality without a religious foundation simply holds no support.

The Bible not only gives a historical accounting of the beginning of time. It also gives us an accounting of the birth and life of Jesus Christ. Even though man has translated the Scriptures from another language, the message remains the same. The problem is that we spend a great deal of time trying to make those words support our changing lifestyles. I have heard people quote the Bible to support their racism against African Americans and Muslims. I have heard people quote the Bible to support their beliefs about a woman's place in the world. The Bible can be used to support just about anything we want it to. We can even interpret the same scripture in different ways. But the scriptures were saved all these many years and studied by many scholars and teachers because the message is still true for us today. It is a message of how to love other human beings and how to live together on this earth. That's it, it is a simple message. There is no hatred and no instructions for evil.

The Bible is the only documentation that we have of the history of man's beginning and life after the birth of Christ, therefore we must believe that it is all true. To that end, unfortunately, man has tried to reinterpret and change the bible to fit into his own personal doctrine and his own personal beliefs. Consequently, as a people, we are confused disillusioned, and lost in a world where there are no clear guidelines, rules, or laws for morality.

An example of our confusion is that there are many different churches under the umbrella of Christianity but each one has its own doctrine and belief system. Some take the Bible literally and if you deviate from the words of the Bible, you are living in sin. There are some churches that take some of the words literally and bend other words to fit into their lifestyles. Some just make it up as they go. Some churches have developed "traditions" and "Styles" that soon get so confused by the parishioners, that they believe that God commanded it so. I was listening to a popular talk show when a woman called in to say that she did not like another woman because the other woman was not of her faith. The talk show host asked her what was her faith? The woman said she was a Christian, but her friend was a Catholic.

The average person is uneducated and uninformed when it comes to religion. Most of us just join a church because we feel comfortable there or we like the preaching, our friends go there, our parents went there, or for any number of other reasons. But rarely do we study or try to understand the doctrine of the church that we are about to join before we join. I have a friend who has told us that her church does not have a doctrine. Webster states that a doctrine is a "teaching instruction", a principle or position or the body of principles in a branch of knowledge or a system of belief, karma or dogma, the principal excepted by a body of believers. It is the belief system of that group of worshipers that constitute a doctrine. I am not that familiar with what I believe to be her church's doctrine, but these are some of the things that I have heard her discuss. "Women are not allowed to serve as elders or deacons." Other churches do have women who are elders or deacons and that constitutes their doctrine. "Women are only allowed to teach young children." She says this is not doctrine but biblical. I say who cares in the big scheme of things. If you choose a church where a woman cannot be an elder or deacon, then go in peace. I am not mad with you. This is the way you choose to worship.

I am not concerned about the doctrine of churches or believers. I am concerned about the dogma. (Not wanting to learn and explore). I am not concerned that one church might believe in worshipping on Saturday instead of Sunday. I am not concerned that each of us may see church differently. My concentration is on how people live what they know and have learned about God. What God expects of us and has in store for us. I don't want to get into whether one doctrine is better than another one. I will not make comments on whether one doctrine or another is true for me. I will use scripture to support my beliefs and ideas. The scriptures I choose may mean something different to you. I don't think that's important in the big scheme of things either.

I use the scriptures of the holy bible to make and express my viewpoints and ideas. My philosophy is not necessarily based on just the holy bible. My ideas could easily express those held in the Holy Koran for example. The Holy Bible happens to be the book that I am most familiar with. While I believe in Christ and Christianity, I do not discount Judaism, Islam or Buddhism, or other organized religions that hold the same ideals and philosophy as I do. My philosophy of life comes from my heart, my life experiences and hopefully, God directed. I do not force my beliefs and ideas on anyone. If my viewpoints and ideas make you think and analyze your own philosophy then "I fought a good fight, I have finished my course, and I have kept the faith" (11 Timothy 4-7)

TABLE OF CONTENTS

INTRODUCTION

I was raised in a home where the kids were sent to Sunday school each Sunday. We were not taken to Sunday school as many children are these days. Your parents didn't have to make you go it was expected of you. That's why older people like to brag about having walked miles to school or church. Parents didn't get the car out just to take the kids to church. We went to a church that was in our community. The only time we went to the regular grown-up church service was on Easter or other special occasions. On those occasions, we could ride in the family car that is if your family owned a car. A lot of people in our community didn't own cars in those days.

I remember walking to Sunday school with my two brothers and stopping to swing on a pole near the corner. I would swing around and around wearing a dress. I remember playing hooky, once in a while, and spending the nickel I had for Sunday school on ice cream or candy. I remember my teachers at the Sunday school, who made it interesting for me. I would go home and tell my parents all about my lesson. I have very fond memories of Sunday school in general. I rarely hear that expression anymore. Sunday school, I think they call it church school now.

My father left our home while I was very young. I do not remember a religious influence coming from him. I don't remember him ever attending church anywhere at any time. I don't remember hearing him pray about anything. That is not to say that he wasn't a God-fearing, man because we never know what is in the hearts of anyone. I was young and don't remember if he left on Sunday to go anywhere. That's why I don't judge him. My mother was never a regular church-going woman either, even after she married my stepfather who was a Baptist minister. I knew she was deeply religious or faithful to God because of the way she lived her life. She was always the one in the neighborhood who looked after the elderly. She was the first person to volunteer to help or serve on various charities. She worked for the Cancer Society handing out leaflets and talking to people about getting help for over twenty-seven years without pay. I watched her care for other people's children, family members who needed her and I watched her travel across town to take an elderly lady to the doctor regularly. She was rarely compensated for her efforts, but she was always the one that people depended upon. She is my example of a person who walks the walk. She never preached or talked about the bible out loud to me. I never heard her quote scriptures or praise the Lord out loud. But there was a bible always nearby and I knew that she was familiar with it. The pages were worn and frayed.

My love for gospel music came from hearing my mother sing while she worked. Some of her favorites were songs that she sang so often when I was a child, that I have retained the words even until today. Such songs as, "What a friend we have in Jesus" and "In the Garden" were basics in my home as I grew up. When she wasn't singing, she played the record player and I learned to love Mahalia. My mother family's religious background was mixed. There was a cousin who was a Catholic nun and another cousin who was a bishop of the Episcopalian church. My mother remembered attending the Episcopalian church as a child back in Spokane, Washington where she was born. My mother is now gone after 93 years to be with Jesus, but her memory is one of a person or Saint who walked the walk.

I attended a Catholic school for a while and anyone my age that attended a Catholic school can attest to the evil and mean actions of many of the sisters. I realize now that these women had never had children of their own and perhaps their tolerance level was extremely low for children. I remember clearly being embarrassed in front of the class on many occasions. I was slapped by the nuns for an infraction, for not bringing homework. I remember having my hand slapped with a board by the nun in front of the class for not spelling a word correctly. I became so traumatized by the experience that my mother had to remove me from that school and return me to public school. I continued to attend Catholic Church and classes for catechism but stopped short of making my first communion. Off and on throughout the years, I attended the Catholic Church with friends and the Baptist church with my mother and stepfather. My new stepfather was a Baptist minister and my brothers, and I was obligated to attend his church more often than we would have liked. The services were always long hot and noisy. But the music was wonderful.

Years later when I married my Junior high school sweetheart, we attended a conversion class at the Catholic church. As adults, we had many questions. The priest leading the class would leave us cold with answers like, "You just have to believe because that is the way it is". Of course, he was talking about faith. We were too young and without understanding at the time. Eventually, my husband and I drifted away and started attending a Presbyterian Church near our home. For the next 25 years, we became hard-working members of the Presbyterian Church. Our children attended both Sunday school and church services. We went to church as a family. Both my husband and I served as Deacons and eventually, we were ordained as Elders. We were also Youth Directors and served on numerous committees. One committee was to hire a new minister. We were totally involved in our church home.

Over the years our attitude began to change about the church as the center of our lives. Our church went through a migration period. The white people began to leave the community because African American families were moving into the neighborhood. Even the white pastor found a reason to leave This can shake your faith when the church is what you have invested your total life in. Then our church went through a huge drop in membership, and it was difficult to attract good pastors. But we were willing to stay for the long haul. There was one white woman left on the Board who refused to turn the church documents and information over to the new members. The new members were all African Americans. The woman started doing very unchristian-like things. She hid the books from the other Board members, she spent church money the way she wanted to, and she caused many new members to leave the church. She did all of this with the support and knowledge of the greater body or administrative body of the Presbyterian Church. She kept in contact with them and was able to convince them that she alone was right and everybody else was wrong. She was the one who found fault with every minister of African American descent that applied. Not one was good enough for the church. So, the pulpit stayed empty for about a year. We had only, visiting ministers which kept the church in an unsteady position. This one woman controlled the church funds until it was forced to close, and she even planned and organized the last service. This was not a phenomenon in those days to just one church. It was happening all over the city of Los Angeles to presbyterian churches and perhaps other denominations as well. The presbyterian church was previously known for its social standing in the community. It was known for standing up during the

70s for black power and other social injustices but when it came to personal membership and local churches, racism was alive and well.

Other things began to prey upon our minds regarding the church as the center of our lives. We could not plan as a family, activities such as vacations or weekends away from home unless we first checked the church calendar. When you are that involved in the church, your life becomes secondary to the life of the church. When our home church closed, we joined another Presbyterian Church where our friend was the preacher. This man was raised in the Baptist Church and preached like a Baptist, and we liked the difference. This church was mostly African American families and much more stable.

Presbyterians are known to be dry preachers because they usually have to have a Master's degree or better. Their high intellect often keeps them from being spontaneous and emotional like a lot of other preachers. This is not to say that emotional preachers don't have degrees, I am sure that many do, in fact, I know many that have their degrees. But Presbyterians are known for their intellectual approaches to life and how we live it. They tend to do more teaching and instructing from the pulpit. I rather liked the change of a preacher who shouted and paced back-and-forth across the pulpit.

We served at the new church much as we had at the old church. Our daughters were married at the new church. Then the preacher friend who had promised to stay at the new church forever took a more lucrative and larger church out of the state where he remained for years before his death. We were devastated because once again we felt the church let us down.

The one thing that kept our faith during those years was a trip that we took to the Holy Land. We traveled to Israel and traced the steps of Christ. We traveled to Egypt and other places that had great religious significance for us. We were baptized in the river Jordan very near where Christ was baptized. We saw with our own eyes things we had only read about in the Bible. Suddenly the Bible took on a more powerful meaning. It wasn't just faith that we had in the book, but we found evidence and truth that we could believe in. We also saw other religions centered in Israel. Most of the major religions of the world have some connection to the Holy Land. We visited Mosques that had religious significance for both Christians and Muslims. We visited a location that had religious significance for Catholics, Protestants, and Muslims. Wow! The only thing that I could say was that everybody's probably got it right. There is something holy here. Perhaps we just interpret it differently.

All of this was occurring during the times that several huge television evangelists were getting caught for having sex in motels with prostitutes and stealing church money. There were Catholic priests getting caught for molesting children and assistant preachers breaking away and starting their own churches. A famous minister had just poisoned his entire flock of nine hundred people, over on foreign soil. This was a time when those things religious that were important to our lives were coming undone. The church had been the center of our existence up until that point. I wasn't unhappy at my new church because our pastor friend left, I was unhappy because they could not replace him. His style was unique, and we had come to enjoy it and look forward to hearing him preach on Sundays. Some of these events brought consciousness to how we view our faith and religion in general. We eventually stopped attending the new church and started visiting other churches. We visited several African Methodist churches and found great enjoyment at the services. We visited several community churches before we decided to settle on an African Methodist Episcopal church to join. Some of the churches we visited required the perishers to bring the money to the front and place it in baskets. This was a turn-off for me. One church locked the doors during collection for fear they would get robbed, they said. Some churches are so big that you must stand outside for an hour earlier just to get in.

We had difficulty finding a home church because that is what we have always been trained to do. What has happened to the church, I mean the real church? The body of people who come together to worship and praise God? The church of people who are true believers? What, I found were huge corporations that put a weekly show on to entertain the hundreds of people who get all dressed up to attend. Corporations with the ability to weed out 10% of a lot of people's incomes. I realize that the Bible speaks of tithing, but what becomes of the 10%? These corporations only feed the emotions and fears of the attendees.

It is easy to find a church where you can sit on the pews every Sunday, and no one would ever know your name. There are churches where you could go to get attention by putting on your own performance. There are churches that brag about their celebrities and show off their important people. There are churches that are in competition to build the biggest and most powerful buildings or plants in the community. There are churches whose fame is made by television or the radio.

Let us talk about the reason for the church? I found many scriptures describing what God meant by the church. I also found scriptures where Jesus spoke about his church. I read some of Paul's letters to the churches and our churches today do not look like any of those descriptions. Over time, man has redesigned the church, so to speak, to meet his own needs. The church is now a building and not a body of people. "We go to church". We should be the church which means “wherever two or three gather together in His name, there God will be also”, that’s what God meant by the church.

What are churches really doing for the community? Some are building senior housing and that’s a nice start, but let's be realistic, housing is a business. A lucrative one, I might add. Some are giving out free food they got from the government or clothes given by the members. What is the church really doing for the community? The money that goes into the building of these monstrous churches could go into a manufacturing company that would put hundreds of people to work. The money that goes into keeping up most church buildings could be going to provide training for people without skills. The church is letting people down in every way possible. The church is good at talking the talk on Sunday morning, but I challenge them to start walking the walk.

Chapter 1
TALKING THE TALK

"Even, the righteousness of God which is by faith in Jesus Christ unto all them that believe: for there is no difference. For all have sinned and come short of the glory of God:"

Romans 3:22

There is a relative who likes to quote the Bible at every opportunity. Every religious family must have someone who is more versed in the words of their faith and who is quick to use it against the rest of the family. For example, my relative uses it to make her appear Stronger. She quotes the Bible verse to back her up as if that gives her the upper hand. She can roll verse after verse after verse so quickly sometimes you don't really understand what she's saying. When she can't find anything else to say she throws final indignation at you "Praise God", and "Glory to the Lord". This relative will sooner cut off her arm than to miss church on Sunday, prayer meeting on Wednesday, and Choir on Thursday. I called this talking the Talk because when it comes to being just a good person, she is a "snake in the grass". She's the one that you must watch out for because she'll tell all your business. Her husband is the one who likes to brag that "God is good", but recently we have found out that he beats his wife and mentally abuses his children.

Another person I know gives exactly ten percent of her income to the church for her tithes. She also attends church every Sunday but maybe not as religiously as the other lady does. This person is so deep into the dogma of her specific denomination that she refuses to listen to anything that might change her mind. She has said over and over "I will never leave my church". Over the years I heard her complain about the pastor, complaints about the way the Sunday school is run, and complaints about some of the things that they preach at her church, but she stands firm, "I will never leave my church". This is an example of becoming a mental slave to tradition. I called this talking The Talk.

Some of us know or have heard of a preacher, pastor, priest, or rabbi who had difficulty keeping their covenant as men of the cloth. I had a friend who was married to a very popular preacher. Their church was a very popular church and people came just to hear the silky voice of a minister who sang most of his sermon. I was very impressed with him when I visited the church. But he had not been at the church more than a year when the wife began to tell me about a female preacher who came to town, supposedly out of nowhere. Her husband, the pastor brought the woman into the church to preach. She set up on the pulpit with him against the wishes of the elders of the church, who had difficulty verifying her credentials. The pastor started dating the woman and spending Sunday afternoons with her and her child. Everybody knew about it in the church because gossip flies quickly. This was probably the most blatant demonstration of a fallen preacher that I have ever seen. His wife sat in the audience on Sunday mornings watching the two of them on the stage singing and praising the Lord. Eventually, that preacher left his wife and church and moved away location unknown.

We have all known the people, who dress the best in church and cry, scream and sometimes fall out every Sunday. These people carry Bibles everywhere they go and can quote verses instantly at your request. Then go home and curse, (but excuse themselves to the Lord above) and then scream at their kids, husband, or neighbor, do evil against others, and pray over every meal they eat. This is really a good example of talking the talk.

This book is not an indictment against the church, the temple or the synagogue, or the good people who attend there. (Acts 20:28) "Take heed therefore unto yourselves, and to all the flock, over the which the Holy Ghost hath made you overseers, to feed the church of God, which he has purchased with his own blood". I believe the modern-day organized place of worship is an important part of our society. It gives families a center and a focus for their moral teaching and understanding. It is a place of solace when there is nowhere else to go. It is the place where we come together with others who believe as we do. "For where two or three are gathered together in my name, there I am in the midst of them" (Matthew 18:19).

We need the instruction of those who have studied more diligently than we have in order to form our own personal beliefs. Our religious leaders are more skilled at teaching the doctrine of their studies in a way that we can understand it. There are many religious leaders who are faithful to their words and who live their lives with character and high morals. My point is that attending church is the act of talking the talk" but how you live your life and use what you have learned is the act of walking the walk.

Walking the walk is more difficult than it sounds because you have to separate out what is the church and what is your personal commitment to God. The two are entirely different because that which you hear in Church comes from a man who has interpreted it for you in a specific style or doctrine. Anytime you receive learning you get an interpretation from the teacher or writer. This book is an interpretation of what I believe. That does not mean that the message is wrong. The message can be correct and hearing it should prepare you for how you will live out the rest of your days on this earth.

Some say that people of cloth preach, teach and instruct with directions from God. This may very well be true but every man sins, and falls short of God. (Romans 3:22) (Hebrews 10:26) "For if we go on sinning deliberately after receiving the knowledge of the truth, there no longer remains a sacrifice for sins," l listen and I try to find learning in what I hear, but I decide what enhances my life and whether it is in the direction that God would have me go. God gave each of us the ability to choose between right and wrong and between that, which is good and that, which is evil. No man or woman can make that choice for you. If you choose to follow the wrong path, you have no one to blame but yourself. Choose wisely and use the God-given independent ability to make your life what you want it to be and your life after death will not be something to worry about.

We must decide how we want our tithes for God spent. Now don't get me wrong, I understand clearly that churches must pay bills, including the pastor, the insurances, and several other obligations. I believe that members of churches are obligated to support the needs of the church. Now, what are the needs? That is the question you need to ask yourself. Does the church take care of its elderly? Does the church give scholarships to their students? Does the church take care of the homeless or even provide blankets, food, and clothing? Does the church have a huge building with empty rooms that no one uses and yet there are homeless people sleeping in the streets? How is your own family doing? Do you have family members in need, but you take your spare money and give it to the church?

So here we are with choices, do you feel guilty because you don't give ten percent to a church that does not walk in the way Jesus did? Then you need to understand why you feel the guilt because walking with God should be your goal and no other. Your choices mean that you can choose to look good among men or look good to God. These choices are yours to make.

Chapter 2
BEARING WITNESS

"Jesus said, "if I bear witness to myself, my witness is not true"

John 5: 31

We teach our children almost from birth that it is important to our lives to impress other people. We care what others think of us and we always want others to like us. That's the way we meet friends and obtain jobs. We want other people to bear witness to who we are. The feedback that we get is often what leads us to have the belief system that we have. If I try to impress you by dressing a certain way and in fact, you are not impressed, I will feel hurt or sad. Sometimes I will try again or maybe not. What I feel about the experience is what develops my thinking about you and me. I may decide that you are not worth much trouble and just ignore you, or I may decide that I am not worthy of your friendship, or I may want to try to impress you again. Each time I fail, I develop a new chain of ideas about you and me. With children, these chains of events can become, the foundation for the way they view the world in general. After all, everyone the child meets represents the world to them. Over the years, we either continue to care about impressing others or we just give up on it altogether.

Whether or not you set out to impress others, just being in the world and living your life touches other people. You may only meet the mailman accidentally one day when you happen to come out on your front porch, or you may have an occasion to speak to the grocery store man because your bread was stale. Whomever you, make contact with, on a daily basis. is the person that you leave your impression with. This is how you are viewed in the world. We have a relative that we hate to talk to because every time we hear from that relative, they have a complaint. They will want to talk for hours about their aches and pains. We often avoid telephone calls because we already know what they want to talk about. The impression made by this relative to the family is that they are to be avoided as much as possible.

Impressions may not be truthful, but ("Let your light so shine before men, that they may see your good works, and glorify your Father which is in heaven".) We live our lives so that men will know us. (Matthew 5:16) We should not set out to create an impression upon others because if it is phony, they will know. Impressions are what others feel about you. Impressions are personal but could be influenced by others who know you well. You should not set out to fool people. We have friends who spend a great deal of money on clothes, cars, houses, and other visual trappings. They hope to give the impression that they are rich. Maybe people will think they are rich. This is simply, "Talking the talk". This is an impression that holds only value in the world but no value in God's eyes. The impression that we want to leave with others is associated with how we want to live among others in this world. If you want to rise above the needs of selfishness, then the impression we want to leave is how we live our lives or how we "Walk the walk".

I am often surprised at what people think of me. I am not always happy about what people think of me, but I have no control over how they view me. More often, than not, what they hear me say and see me doing does create their view of me. Their view of me is often what they see at a distance. How I look and act physically. When I was coaching girls' basketball, people saw a gray-headed lady, slightly heavy surrounded by girl basketball players. I have no idea what they must think of that picture, but I assume they think I must have been a gym teacher during my working years and now I am continuing my work at the local parks. Not true. I am retired, know very little about basketball, but I like working with children. If I meet someone for the first time, whatever I am doing or saying at that instance will become a legacy to man. First impressions are difficult to erase unless that person becomes a true friend and discovers the true person in you. That is what it is like when you care what others think of you. My only concern is what I think of me and what God thinks of me. I want someone to look at me and say, Gee, I wish I had the time to work with the youth like she does. Perhaps someone will be inspired to help children someday because they remembered the gray-headed woman. These are the only concerns regarding the impressions I want to leave on this world. If I live my life in such a way as to please God, then I have walked the walk and no amount of "lip service" can destroy that.

Bearing witness in the biblical sense is similar to what we think of other people and ourselves. When you love God and have understanding you will speak well of God. That does not mean to spend your time preaching or talking the talk. You will want to make sure that you are representative of a person who believes in God. In proverbs, Solomon says 7:16 "these six things doth the Lord hate; yay, seven are an abomination unto him: A proud look, a lying tongue, and hands that shed innocent blood. A heart that deceives, wicked imaginations, feet that be swift in running to mischief, a false witness that speaks lies, and he that soweth discord among brother." When we seek to impress, these are the values and characters of a person who does not walk the walk.

Chapter 3
FAITH

“The apostle said unto the Lord, increase our faith. And the Lord said, if you have faith as a grain of mustard seed, yea, he might say onto this sycamore tree, be thou plucked up by the root, and be thou planted in the sea; and it should obey you”.

Luke’s 16: 5

These are probably the most overworked words in the human language "Just have faith”. Most people have no clue what faith really means. Faith is the key to the power that God gave to man. Man must overcome his own vulnerabilities if he or she is to harness the power of faith. Faith is just a word, but it means to trust and believe. Trust is a word to describe the feeling that is complete and without a doubt. Belief is based on what you know and understand of something. Based on knowing and understanding, you make a conscious choice to believe. Both of these, human reactions require complete obedience and control over the human mind and body. Very few men or women have experienced this total giving over the soul and spirit that we call faith. We can read about such people in the Bible and other religious writings. There was of course Abraham who was willing to kill his only son because God asked him to. There was David who slew the giant because he knew God was on his side. There are many stories in the Bible of people who have faith and because of their true faith were rewarded for it. But modern-day people cannot achieve the same kind of thing because we have already destroyed our belief in the possible.

A Centurion sent friends to get Jesus to save a dying man. When Jesus arrived, the Centurion decided that his house was not worthy of Jesus. He asked Jesus to just say that the man was healed, and he would believe that it was done. Jesus said in Luke 7:9. "I say unto you I have found no greater faith, no, not in Isreal".

How many times have you prayed for something to happen or not happen and the moment the words came out of your mouth, something creeps into your mind that says, "Well if it does not happen, I'll do something else". How many times have you prayed for something, and your mind immediately thought, it is impossible, but I'll pray anyway? Not only does your mind erase your prayer but we sometimes go back and pray for the same thing again. Sometimes again and again. This behavior is not of faith. Faith requires complete utter belief that whatever you ask of God, it will be done. That is the power that the average man can achieve. However, many say we must pray and ask for the same thing, over and over again until we receive it. This is a contradiction for me.

I sit at my desk thinking that if God said," with such as much faith as a mustard seed that I could move mountains" then I could make one million dollars appear right in front of me. Right here on my desk. One million dollars. My mind immediately responded with "That is a total impossibility". Therefore, it was totally impossible for me to make that happen. That is what I mean about men being unable to have that kind of belief system because we have already decided what was possible and impossible. God can read your thoughts.

Faith is believing in something so strong that you stake your life upon it. No, I cannot think of anything in this world I would stake my life on. I love my family with all my heart, but I know that they are only human and will fall short of being perfect every time. If I stake my life on one of them, It, would be completely out of love because in the back of my mind, I would be saying, "Suppose they let me down?" But God is different if you have faith. He made a promise that he would never let us down. Your belief system must be totally without a doubt. We are always willing to do the" Talk" but when it comes to a demonstration of our faith, we fall short. We cannot make a million dollars appear because we don't believe it can happen. But I say to you, if you really had the faith that it takes, it is possible. Nothing will be out of reach. You could move mountains.

Paul says (Corinthians 5:6) "Therefore we are always confident, knowing that, whilst we are at home in the body, we are absent from the Lord; (for we walk by faith, not by sight") You might wonder why I don't own one million since I have discovered the secret to God's graces. I, like you, have been so socialized since the day I was born that it is extremely difficult for me to exhibit the kind of faith I speak of. However, I am trying to teach myself to increase my faith, not by my words but by my actions. So, I go to God and ask. Asking is another problem for me because I was raised to believe I should never ask anyone for anything. That was my parent's pride. They did not want anyone to know that they could not provide everything that I needed. Pride is often false and does not serve us well.

God said clearly, "Ask, and it shall be given to you, Seek and you shall find, Knock, and it shall be opened on to you" (Matthew 7:7) A good way to exercise your ability to increase your faith is to ask God for something that is easy to ask. Something that will not make your mind wander into whether it is possible or not. Something so simple that you do not have to think of it again. Almost immediately if you're mind has not erased the request, you get a feeling that it has been done. When it actually, happens and you can see it or feel it, your elation will be so intense that it will heighten and strengthen your faith.

(Matthew 18:19) Jesus says, "Verily I say unto you, whosoever ye shall bind on earth shall be bound in heaven; and whatever ye shall be bound in heaven: Again, I say unto you, That, if two of you shall agree on earth as touching anything that they shall ask, it shall be done for them of my Father which is in heaven. For where two or three are gathered together in my name there am I in the midst of them" (Matthew 8:18) Jesus talks about power in numbers. He says if two or more agree in my name, it shall be done. Now for me that means that I need to surround myself with righteous people so that my power would be increased. If I am working towards harnessing the power that God has given me then I need to be doing that every day of my life. That would require that everyone around me would be working for the same purpose. If you surround yourself with negative people who have no faith in God, then it stands to reason that your power will be decreased rather than increased. Negativity increases the amount of doubt that you store in your brain or mind. When you pray, those doubts creep in and eliminate your prayer. Your faith must be pure, clean, and without a doubt. When you go to the Lord you must not have any negative thoughts or vibes about God's power. You just ask one time and know that it will be done. Doubt will make you think of it again which will erase your request.

Many of us know people that are not good for us, but we don't want to hurt their feelings. We keep these so-called friendships that hurt us because we don't have the courage to stay away from them. A person who is evil or negative will only cost us pain. It is our duty as a believer in God to try and help our friends or relatives to find inner peace and the love of God. But if you fail, you must move away from that person and not allow their negativity to bring doubt into your life. (Proverbs 14:7) "Go from the presence of a foolish man, when thou perceive not in him the lips of knowledge".

Chapter 4
PRAYER

"And when thou pray, thou shall not be as the hypocrites are; for they love to pray standing in the synagogues and in the corners of the streets, that they may be seen of men. Verily I say unto you, they have their reward. But thou, when thou prayest, enter into thy closet, and when thou hast shut thy door pray to thy Father which is in secret; and thy Father which see in secret shall reward thee openly. But when ye pray, use not vain repetitions, as the heathen do; for they think that they shall be heard for their much speaking".

Matthew 6:5

In the New Testament, Jesus tells us how to pray and he gives us the "Lord's Prayer". (Matthew 9:13) "Our father which, art in heaven, hallowed be thy name. Thy kingdom come, thy will be done in earth, as it is in heaven. Give us this day our daily bread. And forgive us our debts, as we forgive our debtors. And lead us not into temptations but deliver us from evil; for thine is the kingdom, and the power, and the glory, forever A-men".

There are many mentions of prayer in the Old and New Testaments of the Bible. Prayer is the way we communicate with God. It is sent to God in Faith. God understands our needs and therefore if you believe in God, you will not have needs. You don't have to beg for anything from God because begging is a form of distrust and unfaithfulness. When we pray, we simply ask God to forgive us our sins and help us to live better. We pray for our friends, our family, and our neighbors that they may have peace and joy in their lives. Never assume you know what is in their hearts. Just pray for them.

I don't care how you manage to re-interpret these Commandments from Jesus. It says what it says. If you stand up and pray on the street corners you have your rewards. Now many would say that the Lord told us to go out and preach the word. Many religions do. There are several religions that go out and knock, on doors, to preach the word. This is also biblical and I do not believe that they are making a "spectacle of themselves", in fact, I think they are being faithful to their belief or doctrine. They may be a nuisance to some people when they knock on your door, but you cannot deny their faithfulness. Preaching and teaching the Word of God anywhere is permitted and demanded of Christians. Let us not confuse praying for our salvation and teaching or reaching others to tell them about the Goodness of our Lord and Savior.

Prayer is an individual thing. It isn't important to demonstrate to anyone that you pray. It isn't important for you to know who is praying and who is not. If you are in a gathering, and, someone asks you to pray, then pray. if you choose to pray or not the prayer must come from the heart and not the mind. Don't pray because someone asked you to. You must pray when you feel the need and no matter where you are when you feel the need, prayer out loud is simply talking the talk.

I recognize that prayer in numbers has more power and that when we pray together, it is out loud. I do not want to confuse prayer given in a large group or during a worship service with prayer by an individual. Organize group prayer has tremendous power. I'm trying to make the case for individuals to understand that prayer should not be done in an automatic fashion. There should be thought and purpose behind it because God will answer prayer.

At one time, I wondered why I did not receive exactly the request I made of God. Sometimes it will make your faith weak if you do not understand how that works. Remember man created technology in a world with all kinds of pitfalls and traps that get us into trouble. For example, we go out and make $10,000 worth of bills and ask the Lord to help us pay them off. You expect the Lord to give you the money to pay all those bills and if he does not, you are disappointed. The Lord promises us peace, joy in our lives, and comfort. He promises to give us what we need. When we ask for tangible things, that is not what we need to survive, the Lord may see it as greed or something that you want because you want it. You got yourself into debt and you must get yourself out of debt. The prayer that you need is the prayer that asks "God to lead you, guide you, and comfort you in your hour of need. You want to amend your ways and try to do better". Then you are not only asking for help, but you are willing to stop the behavior that gets you into trouble in the first place. God helps those who help themselves. (By the way that is not biblical). Now if you have real faith in your heart, you can ask for a million dollars, it will be done. Prayer is a tool that we use to communicate to our father, which is in heaven. If you make a prayer request of God and continue to act or feel sad about it because you haven't received your request, you are erasing your request. Another example is if you are depressed because you don't have your rent money and then you ask God for the rent money, You have to stop being depressed because God made a promise to you that he will give you what you ask if you only have a little faith. (Mathew 7:7) "Ask and ye shall receive, Seek and ye shall find, Knock and it shall open". The moment you ask God for whatever it is, you cannot continue to worry about it. Because God made a promise to you that he will give you what you ask for. Sometimes he fulfills the request instantaneous, sometimes he chooses the date and time, and sometimes he makes the request bigger than you could ever imagine. But if he promised it, he will deliver it. It may not be in the form of your request, but he will make it right.

I believe that God will send a human or a pet to fulfill your request sometimes. We must be open to see that when our lives turn for the better, it was God. Only God can know what would make your needs complete. Who would guess that a pet would cure loneliness or a stranger would change how you see the world. Only God can do that for you, but you must believe. Likewise, you could be the blessing that God sends to someone praying. That's a thought we often miss.

A smile should appear on your face because you know that God will answer your prayer. You do not have to keep begging or making that request again, but you should continue to pray for God to give you the strength to carry on. When praying, on a daily basis, just ask God to forgive you of your sins. Repeat the Lord's prayer. Tell the Lord what is going on in your life and how much you need him. Talk to him, but then you must do the walk by yourself.

Chapter 5
MORALITY

"Thou mayest walk in the way of good man and keep the paths of the righteous"

Proverbs 2:20

Morality comes from what we learn from our religious leaders, the holy Scriptures, the laws of our land, and what we know in our hearts to be the right thing. That is an oversimplification of what morality is, in reality, morality is what is simply the right thing to do. Modern society has muddled the clear description of morality. We have pushed the line, so to speak, from what was a clear guideline to a political guideline of morality. For people who believe in God my example is the Bible, then morality is clearly defined for you. There is no place in the Bible that gives you the right to change it to be more moderate. There is no place in the Bible that gives you the right to stretch what it says to make it more feasible. I have heard the arguments and believed them myself at one time. That the Bible is simply a story that gives us a guideline to live by. That it was never meant to be taken literally. That it was never meant to be applied to Modern Times. I tell you that if you have the ability. to manipulate the Bible to meet your personal beliefs, then nothing else in the Bible is true. Either one sentence is incorrect. or all the sentences are incorrect. There is no room in the Bible for flexibility. The 10 Commandments are clear. Thou shall not. It does not say, sometimes you can and sometimes you can't. It is clear. Thou shall not kill. Would we allow someone in our society to get away with murder because the Bible did not mean it literally? Otherwise, we would not have to have a law against murder. The law against murder is a form of society's morality. We need to have order in society so that people will act decently towards one another. So, we apply laws that have moral value. “Thou shall not covet thy neighbor’s wife.” We have moral laws against adultery.

I have heard people say that we cannot legislate morality, but I beg to differ with them. Morality laws are those laws that make us do the right thing according to the Scriptures. The legislature can pretend that they are separate from the church but that is not true. We use morality in our governance of people as a thermometer of truth and faith in our government. Sometimes our legislators try to ignore morality so that they can steer clear of religious values. Separation of church and state is a fallacy. We often try to bend away from the morality issues to try and accommodate large numbers of people who use politics to make others follow their beliefs. I personally have no thoughts, nor do I make any judgment calls about what others choose to do in their lives. But I refuse to close my eyes and pretend that God didn't mean what he said.

We have come to believe that it is all right to have sex and children outside of marriage. None of these things are frowned upon in our society today. They have become so natural and so acceptable that churches are afraid to make a judgment regarding them. Preachers, steer clear of preaching about people living together out of wedlock or having children out of wedlock. People get married every day in the church who have been living in sin for years. While this seems to be the best way to resolve a bad situation, it puts the church in a position of support for unwed couples. It makes a mockery of the covenant of marriage. Even though the Bible is clear regarding sex outside of marriage. We cannot deny the truth because it hurts. We do our children an injustice when we refuse to stand up and walk the walk when it comes to morality.

Children need to be told to remain free of sex until they marry because that is what God wants them to do. When we give our children birth control, then we say that we do not have faith in you, and we don't trust you. We don't believe that God can help you. We tell our children that if you have a child out of wedlock, then you have a choice. You can just kill the unborn baby and start all over again or you can get a welfare check. We are as much to blame for our unfaithfulness as children who were not given the understanding. (Isaiah 6:2-5) "for as a young man marry a virgin, so shall thy sons marry thee, and as the bridegroom rejoice over thee".

We cannot let the secular world dictate our morality. The Bible stays constant in its message and God's word is constant. Until the end of days, the Bible's message will be the same, but life here on earth may become a place without morality. That does not mean that just because people don't believe anymore that the word has changed. If we continue to follow in the path of unrighteousness, we will still burn in the fire. (Isaiah 10:8) "for wickedness burneth as the fire".

Chapter 6
LOVE AND MARRIAGE

"Owe no man anything, but to love one another: for he that loveth another hath fulfilled the law"

Romans 13-8

The Bible is filled with wisdom regarding love and marriage. The greatest love is a love for God Almighty. The next love is for the neighbor and for thy self. Love is another word we often use without understanding. Sometimes we can't tell the difference between lust, desire, and friendship. Sometimes we confuse all three to mean that we are, "in love".

Love has taken on two different meanings. The first being the love you have for everyone or the people who are the closest to you. The other being the love you have for a lover or sexual partner. The truth is there is only one love and God wants us to love each other no matter who it is. With love comes respect and that is where we fall short. Some years ago, my nine-year-old granddaughter came home from school one day and told me that she had faced her fears. For my family that means when something is scary, we must do it anyway. We face our fears and the fears will go away. I asked her what she meant by that. She stated that she told a boy that she liked him. We don't believe in encouraging boyfriend and girlfriend relationships with nine years old but we don't discourage what is natural. I asked her what she liked about the boy. She didn't know. Perhaps it is the way he walks? I continued. No, she said. Perhaps he is very smart? No, she said, he gets D's and F's in school. Well, I said, it must be something that you like about him. She thought for a while and said, he has curly hair.

I realized that my granddaughter hadn't really connected with the boy in any tangible way. After more conversation, I learned that the boy knocks her books from her desk every time he passes her. We are not sure what his motives are. He didn't knock anyone else's books off. My granddaughter liked the attention the boy gave her. He made her feel special and somehow that was interpreted to mean she liked him. Or, that she was special to him. This behavior is not linked to just nine years old, in fact, many adult women and men get confused about what they feel about another person. Somewhere around 12 or 13, our hormones start kicking in and suddenly we react to sexual stimuli. If we see a movie and two people or kissing or worse nowadays, we get physically stimulated and our bodies react. Girls might experience a discharge in their panties and boys might experience an erection. These two reactions are normal for good healthy humans. The problem comes when young people are not taught to understand what is going on with their bodies. That it is normal, and they often cannot control it and it is expected. There is no shame in that. The problem is they may interpret their reactions to sexual stimulation to mean they have some special attachment to the person who caused the reaction.

These reactions, while normal are considered lustful or desirous. At any age, lustful and desirous reactions must be tempered with self-control. These are the reactions that create physical connections for people. "He turns me on" or "I get so excited when I am around her". Most relationships start with lust or desire as the basis for exploration into romance. Step one is often the jump start of the romance (lust and desire) then the second step is sensation. Sensation is usually smells, touching, dancing, romancing, and kissing. These two steps can last the entire relationship and that is why many relationships last for years, but in the majority of cases, this portion of the relationship is fleeting and lasts for a very short time. Too much familiarity often spoils lust, desire, and sensual feelings. That explains why many relationships fail soon after sexual contact.

Nothing about step one or step two has anything to do with love. Love is the greatest emotion man can give or receive. It is not based on lust, desire, or sensations. Love is based on respect, trust, and human connection at an intellectual level. Friendships between people are also built on mutual respect, trust, and human connection. I describe human connection as the liking of someone. When you like being in the presence of another or like what they say or how they say it. This is a human connection. When people like each other they usually have something in common that keeps the friendship fresh. Common concerns, common lifestyles, or common interests. Sometimes the friendship will just disappear or become dormant when common interests disappear. It is the same when two people become Friends. They also must have common interests to keep the relationship alive. When the friendship is strong, love will have a place to bloom. It is all right for men and women to be just friends and not lovers.

I remember how I use to be when I was a teenager. If young people have sex and anyone found out about it, the girl's reputation was ruined. Nowadays, girls brag about having sex with every guy they know. They wear their sexual life as a badge of honor. Reputation was important to us because it said something about us. There were the good girls. the guys took home to meet their mothers. There were the other girls who the guys prefer to be with because they put out. But everyone knew the guy would never marry the girls who put out. We clearly understood what we had to lose, and we made our choices based on that. We went through the same emotions and feelings the teenagers today are going through. We had to struggle with ourselves to stay virtuous. If a girl got pregnant out of wedlock, then she was sent home to grandma down in Mississippi or somewhere. If she returned to town, she would tell everyone that she was married, and her husband was in the military. Children out of wedlock were not a popular thing in those days.

Times have certainly changed but the Bible stays constant, and God made a man and a woman to be together as a family. Man fertilizes a woman and she makes babies. He becomes a father and she becomes a mother and they constitute a family. Now I am not against other forms of families. I am just making the point that people must be responsible for their sexual choice. We can manipulate nature or God's laws and get away with it while we are on earth because God gave every man free will.

Dating is the process whereby couples learn about each other. Dating is the time when couples talk about who they are and ask questions about who they are dating. Dating is the opportunity for people to get to know each other's families. It is the time to share deep feelings about religion, having children, politics, social issues, and families. It is a time to develop trust, respect, and responsibility. It is not the time to live together and pretend to be married. It is not the time to become intimate and risk having children out of wedlock. When the dating ritual is not taken seriously, the chances of the relationship losing its power are tremendous. Relationships not based on sound judgment and commitment are doomed for failure. The statistics, for divorce is extremely high and it is even higher for persons who first move in together before marriage. The process of moving in together before marriage is the easy way to a relationship. Marriage takes commitment, character, trust, respect, and responsibility. There is no reason to try it out first, if all of those things exist trying it out first is just talking the talk.

Chapter 7
COMMITMENT

"He remembers his covenant forever, the promise he made for a thousand generations"

1 Chronicles 16:15

I have been married to the same man for over 62 years. I will be the first to say that it hasn't always been a bed of roses. There were many days yes, many years where our marriage was less than it should've been. But nevertheless, marriage is a covenant a contract a bond between two people and God. There was always respect and responsibility between us. The two most important elements which keep the marriage together. The marriage covenant is clear, (Mark 10:8) "What therefore God has joined, let no man put asunder, and they twain shall be one flesh: so, then they are no more twain, but one flesh."

Marriage is the most important commitment that people can enter, into therefore do not take it lightly. That is why I believe in dating for a long period of time. Dating is the opportunity to learn about one another. Learning about a person does not mean that you must be intimate or sexual. Sex is the response to desire and lust when it is done outside of the covenant of marriage. Intimacy outside of the marriage means that there is a discussion of intimate things such as personal family matters. Such as personal ideas and thoughts about life and having children. It is a conversation about sex and personal needs. It is conversations about life in general, and in, particular. Intimacy means holding hands, hugging, and liking it.

It means caring and being concerned about another person. It takes a very long time to get to know someone well enough to want to marry them. You know that the two of you are not a perfect matched couple when you cannot talk about any subject in the world. You know you are not a matched couple when you don't like some of the things about the other person. Don't make the mistake of thinking that people change because they change their name or living situation. People are who they are by history. Our character and our belief systems are developed as young children and will not change because of love or any other reason we are who we are.

I met my husband in junior high school and our relationship as friends or girlfriend and boyfriend lasted throughout high school. That was a six-year relationship just getting to know each other. We married much younger than I would recommend for others because it was a real struggle. But the important point I want to make is that when we married, we knew each other's character very well. We liked each other and respected each other's family backgrounds. We took our vows seriously and even though we faltered over the many years, the strong foundation we developed, in the beginning, kept us together. Age has strengthened our resolve and love for one another. We are still happy, still having fun together and now after all these years are just beginning to truly understand love as God wanted it for us.

Commitments are just as important when it comes to our daily lives. We make promises every day and our word is either true or false. If we don't keep our commitments, then eventually others will lose faith and trust in us. We commit by signing contracts making verbal promises to our children our jobs and to our neighbors. Along with commitment is responsibility. Responsibility, in my opinion, is the number one character that I look for in people. A responsible person is a person who lives up to their commitments. God made a commitment or covenant with us, and we must use his example when we make commitments to others.

God was very clear when it comes to divorce, (Mark 10:11) "Whosoever shall put away his wife, and marry another, committed adultery against her. And if a woman shall put away her husband, and be married to another, she committed adultery". Now Jesus was not saying that you had to live together forever. if two people cannot live together in harmony perhaps it is better to live apart in harmony. Remarrying is something that each will have to live with and deal with.

It would be my suggestion that we first take the time it takes to know a person before marrying in the first place. Try to make sure that the feelings that you have for that person are not just lust or desire. The feelings that will sustain a marriage forever are trust, faith, respect, and general friendship. Friendship is very important to people who must live under the same roof, share the same toothpaste and bedroom. Friendship is often underrated as a characteristic necessary for marriage. Friendship means there are common interests, there is respect for who and what the other person does or likes. There is a mutual understanding of who the other person is and what the other person stands for.

Perhaps the most important thing you would want to know about a perspective mate is who and where they come from. Unfortunately, our past often creeps into our futures. If you are clear about the background of your mate and know all about the family and still want to take the other person on, then you do so with all, of the information you need. Your commitment to that person will be based on sound knowledge and not on just feelings and passions.

When commitments fail and a marriage ends in divorce, then we must remain responsible. If there are children involved, then make sure they do not suffer for your mistakes. Be responsible means that you have to put aside your personal "outrage", your personal feelings of hurt, your personal feelings of anger, or whatever it is. You must have enough character to put your children first. Children are made in a committed relationship and your promise to them, at the time they were born, was that they would have a loving family. That means when there is a divorce, rise above the pain and suffering to be responsible toward your children.

In general, making a commitment includes your faith and your obligations to those things that you believe. If your faith is strong and you are walking in your faith then you must give everything you have to stay firm. You cannot back down. If you promise to tithe to the church, then you must follow through. If you promise to help someone, then you must follow through.

Your word must mean something. Your word is your walk.

Chapter 8
LIVING WITH EVIL

"Abstain from all appearances of evil"

Thessalonians 5:22"

"For every one that doeth evil hate the light, neither cometh to the light, lest his deeds should be exposed."

John 3:20

Evil is what we do when we hurt any of God's creatures physically or mentally. Evil is what we do to our children just to get back at our husbands or wives. I see it every day when people divorce and then fight over the children. Each parent trying to turn the children against the other parent. Each parent blaming the other for being a bad husband or wife. Sometimes they blame each other for all of their problems. Eventually, the children believe they are the reason for the divorce. This is evil.

Evil is also when we commit a sin and we know it is a sin. It was when we continue to do the things, we know we should not, but we do it anyway. Evil is harboring bad thoughts about our friends and our neighbors. Evil is harboring bad thoughts about any of God's creatures. Evil is when we purposefully go out of our way to hurt someone. Evil is when we gossip about another person. Evil is when we turn away when others are hurting other people. How many times have you watched evil but you kept your mouth shut because you didn't want to get involve? That is evil.

Webster's Seventh New Collegiate Dictionary says that evil is, "something causing discomfort or repulsion; offensive; disagreeable; causing harm; not good morally; wicked." Well, you get the idea. Even the name "evil" denotes a strong emotion of being bad. I don't believe that most people set out to be or do evil things. However, we do know that some people do set out to hurt others both physically and mentally. The newspapers are full of incidents that are caused by evil people. So, when evil people do evil things, they are usually in denial that they have committed an evil act. Rarely will you hear anyone say, I am so sorry, that was evil of me. Evil is often thought of as something we see in the movies when it is associated with the devil or his demons, because good people cannot be evil.

I preferred to think that evil is an act rather than a person. However, I have known people who never stop being evil, and therefore, they do appear to be evil. The appearance of evil is what we need to avoid. If you hurt another person, that is an evil act. Perhaps you may have an explanation for what you did but it does not erase the fact that it was an evil act. Perhaps you hurt another person in retaliation for something they did to you. It still does not erase the fact that your act was evil as well. Exchanging one evil act for another does not erase the fact that evil occurred.

I knew a woman who had lived an Evil life all her entire existence. This was a woman who had sinned against God's words, against her children, against her friends, against herself. She had committed so many evil acts that she was thought to be evil. I believe this woman had lived such an evil lifestyle for so long that she could not change. She died in her 80s. Her life on earth had been a living hell. Some of her children died violently, some were drugged out somewhere on the streets, and even more are mentally handicapped with alcoholic symptoms. This is a woman who I avoided with everything I knew. When you are faced with evil from another person just walk away. Evil will try to find its way to you without you looking for it.

We all have done evil acts because we will always fall short of being perfect. It is the act of not trying to make amends and learning from our mistakes that keeps the evil in us. If we continue to take the same path that we took before even though it cost us to have the appearance of evil, then we have not learned. We have not tried to walk the walk.

Chapter 9
WALKING THE WALK

"Make you perfect in every good work to do his will; working in you that which is well-pleasing in his sight, through Jesus Christ; to whom be the glory forever and ever. Amen"

Hebrews 13:21

Walking the Walk is simply "being about it and not talking about it". It is action. It is what we do with our lives, not what we hope to do, or dream about, or wish for. Do you support any charities monthly? Do you share your income, or do you store it up in the bank for your rainy day? Do you visit your neighbors, church members, or other persons who need help? Our seniors depend on us to make sure they are all right. Do you care for animals who are at risk or suffering from abuse? Do you support students who are struggling to get through college? God will return your faithfulness in ways you cannot imagine. I have a testimony right here, but I never talk about what I do because it is between me and God. I never want a man to reward me for anything I do. I only want to please God.

The hardest lesson for us to learn in life is wisdom which comes from our age. (Proverbs 8:11) "For wisdom is better than rubies, and all the things that may be desired or not to be compared to it". Young people no longer respect the wisdom of a person who has not only done it, but also been there, saw it, taught it, bought it, lived it, felt it, ate it, gave it, and know it. Young people only know what they possibly could know within the time limit of their young lives. Each year you live, you will experience more. Living then becomes the key to knowledge and wisdom.

We must take care of our physical bodies so that we can live long enough to see what we haven't seen. It is important to stay fit by exercising, eating properly, and seeing the doctor and dentist. We owe our families the right to have us in their lives for as long as possible. We owe our family the least amount of pain and suffering when we leave this world. We must be responsible regarding how we live our lives. I smoked cigarettes for over 20 years. It was a popular cool thing to do. We smoked in the theaters and watched the smoke spiral up into the ceiling. We smoked in the grocery store and the doctor's office and any other place we went. I cannot think of any place where we could not smoke. There were ashtrays everywhere. Today it is not a popular or cool thing to do because we know it kills. If it does not kill us, then it could kill the people around us. So, I stopped smoking. I made a commitment to stay free of cigarettes and I have kept that commitment. Now we are faced with another pandemic and we must do what the doctors and science tell us to do. If not for you, for those you love and those around you.

I believe, "If you don't use it, you lose it". Our mental health is just as important as our physical health. We must keep our minds active by reading, learning, and thinking. We need to learn to be tolerant of people. Tolerance means to give in to the feelings of others and try to understand that you are not always right. Perhaps someone else has a good thought. Perhaps a difference you see in another is a good thing. Being tolerant means to not make judgments against another. Being tolerant means to be kind and caring. We must also learn to be patient. Patience means that others may not think as quickly as you do. Patience means that others may not think the same as you do. Patience means that you will allow another to give an opinion without comment. Patience means that you must wait and give another a chance. We must also learn to be forgiving. Forgiving means that people often do things accidentally. Forgiving means that people often do things unknowingly. Forgiving means that people often do things stupidly. We forgive because we cannot harbor hatred in our hearts. Hatred only hurts us. Hatred cannot hurt anyone else.

There are many attributes that we need to develop to be good people. We need strength, which comes not from our physical abilities but from our mental abilities. Strength means to be able to look problems in the face and still make rational decisions. We need to be happy or at least keep a happy thought and a pleasant smile on our faces. Life often gives us exactly what we ask for. When we are sad or unhappy, most of the time, it will eat us up from the inside and eventually make us ill. Happy thoughts and a smile will help others to make it through the day. Being kind is very important because it helps us to reach outside of ourselves to spread love, as God would have us to do. Simple kindness such as saying hello and goodbye, and make an effort to comment on something nice about another person.

Living in this world is not easy because we are often brought into the world by young and inexperienced parents who have not been given a new baby manual. Consequently, we are accidentally scarred in many ways. However, the scars are usually not permanent if we refuse to let them mark us for life. We must always strive to be good people. Nevertheless, the scars lead us into the individual paths that we take as adults. Humans are different in every way from their parents, from their brothers and sisters, and anyone else in the world. Since there was only one of you ever in this life and on this earth, make the best of it, make it count. Make sure that you leave a legacy behind you for the next unique individual. Make sure that you have been all that you can be. Make sure that you are striving every day to be better than you are today. Make sure that you make mistakes one time that you don't repeat them a second time. Make sure that you read and learn and grow. Make sure that you help your neighbor, your friend, and your family to be the best they can be. Think before you condemn another. Think before you make judgments of another. Think before you decide you know it all. Think before you speak. Think before you pray. If you do these things, you will begin to understand all that God wants for you. Understanding brings knowledge and knowledge is the gift of life. Take one step at a time until one day you will find that it is easy to walk the walk.

"For by one spirit we are baptized into one body, whether we be bond or free; whether we be Jews or Gentiles; and have been all made to drink into one spirit. For the body is not one member, but many."

— **1 Corinthians 12:13**

www.ingramcontent.com/pod-product-compliance
Lightning Source LLC
LaVergne TN
LVHW010507160826
845677LV00012B/2705

* 9 7 9 8 4 9 1 2 5 9 3 0 4 *